LITTLE ANT & THE SHADOW BULLY

written and illustrated by

Ilene Dudek

Dedicated to making the world a better place.

Little Ant & the Shadow Bully
Copyright 2019 by Ilene Dudek. All rights reserved.

Printed in the United States of America by Kindle Direct Publishing, an Amazon company.

No part of this publication may be reproduced, or
stored in a retrieval system, or transmitted in any form or by
any means, electronic, mechanical, photocopying, recording, or
otherwise, without written permission from the author.

ISBN 978-0-578-53171-7

Some shadows are big, some shadows are small,
but what if your shadow was no fun at all?

And every time you walked through town, he made the most embarrassing sounds.

He never liked to hold the door...

And made a mess at the grocery store.

"Naughty shadow, what is your deal?
Why do you like to make little girls squeal?"

He said, "I am dark—and shady too.
I'm a shadow; it's what I do."

The ant said, "Please, don't be so rude.
You need to fix your attitude!"

But the shadow simply wouldn't quit,
and the ant knew it was time to split!

Over mountains and through the grass,
until he was alone at last.

"I did it," he said, "and I feel fine!
I left that bully far behind."

And when the garbage truck passed by,
he launched the shadow through the sky.

"See you later," he said with joy.
"Go find someone else to annoy!"

The ant said, "I really have to know,
why is there trouble everywhere you go?"

The ant said, "I am sorry you are blue, but you can't make others feel bad too!"

The shadow said, "I never knew."

And so, they made a plan that night
to decorate the town with lights.

And the ant invited everyone
to come along and have some fun.

Before they knew it, there would be
shadows as far as the eye could see.

"Look at them all—they're just like me!"

That night, the shadow played and played, and pinky-promised to change his ways!

He said, "I want to be good and kind, and leave my shady past behind."

And the ant could see that it was true.
"I finally found a friend in you!"

Made in the USA
Columbia, SC
06 January 2020

86145587R00018